Alison Dunhill

AS PURE AS COAL DUST

SurVision Books

First published in 2021 by
SurVision Books
Dublin, Ireland
Reggio di Calabria, Italy
www.survisionmagazine.com

Copyright © Alison Dunhill, 2021

Cover image: *WonderCloud* installation by Alison Dunhill
at Norwich Undercroft, 2019
Mesh with Found Metal and LED strip
Photo by Roger Bilder
Copyright © Alison Dunhill, 2019
Copyright © Roger Bilder, 2021

Design © SurVision Books, 2021

ISBN: 978-1-912963-23-2

This book is in copyright. No part of this publication may be reproduced, stored in a retrieval system, or transmitted in any form or by any means without the prior permission in writing from the publisher.

Acknowledgements

Grateful acknowledgement is made to the editors of the following, in which some of these poems, or versions of them, originally appeared:

Joe Soap's Canoe (1992): "January" and "Fragments" (then titled *On the Backs of Sheep in Evening Sun*)

SurVision: "End"

I owe an enormous debt of gratitude to my friend and mentor, the poet Sue Burge, for her ongoing inspiration and incisive evaluation as this current work grew.

And to my partner, Roger, for everything, always.

The title "You Make Me Feel Brand New" is taken from The Stylistics song of 1973.

Contents

Breaking Good	5
Tiger Heron	6
Flying to the Land of Giants	7
Fish Pool with White Columns	8
Accident	10
Niemeyer in Niteroi	12
Cloud Construction	14
Startle	15
Wild	16
Gradients	17
Fragments	18
Life No Bigger	20
Fountain	21
Put Out the Light...	
First Act	22
Intermission	23
End	24
Fiesole in the Bentley	25
October	26
New Door	28
Only Opera	29
January	30
A Table Separates Us	31
Fifteen Hours in Sifnos	32
You Make Me Feel Brand New	34
Salthouse Swans	35
Ice Moon	36

Breaking Good

Brass-edged cactus gardens on marble floors greet us in 'One Mile High City'. Alamo gleams its neon and we follow. In a long night pierced with *please leave your vehicle in neutral* we droop like dead fireweed over the station wagon's high cloth seats. Machine chocolate bars stab the half sleep. At five the sun is lighting the mountains in the west. This dawn is America. Her horizon is spread with scalloped meringue. The sight is so good we break into *O Lord won't you buy me a Mercedes Benz?* Automatic is easy...

Tiger Heron

I saw you
through the bank's bamboo verticals,
your signature decoration flashing,
your movement in stopped strobe.

I saw you
quiet, on the edge of the Amazon. River of majesty,
shining diamonds up
through the parallels of our planked floor.

I saw you
prey-poised, stealthy still,
your leg raised in stylish bend.
I knew the elegant silhouette, but the patterns were strange.

I saw you
a hybrid creature,
cascading and spreading your dress camouflage
in sun's crescents and rhomboids on equatorial leaf and trunk.

Flying to the Land of Giants

Santiago Airport. Landed and stopped on the runway. Twelve hares on the grass island, five small private planes. Ten helicopters. About thirty rabbits. Take-off. Slowly higher. There's no ripple or wave in this snake of brown sludge oozing in elegant belted bends over the land it made fertile. Now, river, you are gargantuan, expanding in patterns of un-river to dark islands, solids in your liquid's mercury. We're not too high in this plane to see the chocolate patches scattered in the green and ochre folds of South America. We're not too high, flying over the Andes foothills, to see the tiny chalk roads wiggling through the desolation of your elephant-skin baby-mountain structure. Your rising peaks. Snow-iced volcanoes; their symmetry formed from central craters; without fire today: *Osorno, Calvoco, Yate*. Secret, compelling, Patagonia.

Fish Pool with White Columns

September 7th, 2014

It's afternoon at the mountain fazenda and the white heron loops and
curves its muscled neck into ampersand, breaking the green river's
    surface with a sloped beak.

Eagles swoop and soar, their wings air-lifted. We are ready to go out
for your birthday dinner. It's a pink evening and night is imminent.

Without warning a lake of water falls from the sky.
Our journey down the mountain is dangerous. What was road ten
    minutes ago

is now fast-currented river, hurling
and swirling the car left, right and mountainside.

The water's power forces us to forty-five degrees.
We bite nails. Flood.

Your driving skills and clear head keep us safe.
Getting out, in foot-clamping mud, drenched, we see

soaked horses fast-dripping water, heads hanging, tails thin,
returning tourists from their ride.

At the restaurant the six of us dry out by the open fire, eat sweet
    palmitos,
fruit and plantain, star-shaped garlic, tender chicken.

We toast you with good wine.
Now on the white sofa the children sleep, curled,

black hair, red hair, Tété, Tiaginho.
The next day in Petropolis we sit by the fish pool as Emperor palms
                                                                                              tower

to the southern hemisphere's moon.
Four white pillars rise on each corner of the pool, four

flower-filled urns sit between and there's a white statue at each corner.
This small symmetrical paradise is calm.

We have stayed an extra day in Petropolis, the imperial city.
Tomorrow, back in Rio, you and I head to Sugarloaf.

You are laden with tripods and cameras.

Accident

September 8th, 2014

This dark mountain track
is the Sugarloaf's body, you say,

not its ancient granite head.
On the concrete tourist promenade

you film-shoot the monkey as it flattens its belly,
legs dangling over, in film star pose,
on the broad branch above us and

above the sun-swooning sea.
Now the forest track is steep, dry-leafed

and root-studded.
Shadows of huge banana leaves, pink flower stars.

We are in Rio looking for insects to film with the close-up lens
I brought out for you on the British Airways flight.

The insects elude us. A moving cable car glints above us, going up,
its metal diagonal line high and silent,

quick-gone. You shoot it.
Its double flashes, a second chrome capsule, going down.

We are in between the two capsules' courses.
Neither up nor down. We cannot board a cable car.

In descent I reject your offered shoulder,
so heavily laden already with tripods and cameras.

(And I am fit.)
I stumble and trip. A giant mahogany root emerges

from the ground. I am now sitting not walking.
This boulder is warm. It's my head.

I am serotonin-happy, but your voice, in command, is just off panicky.
I bleed into the mountain, I am wearing red silk. I can't see the blood at
the back.

You can. Your sweatshirt and the one the Argentinian tourists give, stem
it a bit.
The Argentinians are so kind. They help us. Call the ambulance.

I am carried down strapped to a stretcher. Wobbly.
Talk about Sylvia Plath when the stitches go in.

Niemeyer in Niteroi

September 12th, 2014

There's nobody around.
They're all in the air-cooled shopping mall.
I'm standing in the red box's shade,
my Berlin black and red scarf turbanned to protect the wound,

looking at the Niemeyer mound.
Its symmetrical form curves a white space
in the pure blue of the sky
its white cement fondue oozes up from the ground,

with water around.
About thirty seagulls hover and swoop;
One white heron struts.
The birds prefer this small lake

to the vast glistening sea just there.
The glistening sea. Its sparkling mass
is pierced by a still black jetty
in silhouette

where three men fish. Four herons – now one,
fly wide-white-winged over it.
The sun-swamped, sun-swooning sea
is flanked by horizons of mountains,

hundreds and thousands of mountains.
Pre Africa-land shift mountains.

Over the water, *a cidade maravilhosa*, I think *City of God*
and the favela guys streaming down their mountain to the glistening
sea.

Cloud Construction

Lines of crystals strewn over Wondermesh. Stars in the night sky. Constellations of city lights on 'islands' on a night flight. Wondermesh clouds, plaster and textile clouds, hanging and light-filled, moving in space, their transparency stopped by small bits of consumer waste. Blue clouds, black cloud, in netting or mesh, threads stretched, draped and coiled with flowers and leaves on silk devorée remnants. Mini-clouds in textile-pierced plaster: a flock of flying wall duck-clouds. Nebulous edges of unmoulded plaster, studded with copper pipe, glass beads. Volcanic craters in symmetry. Miniature Doric columns with coloured ribbon-tied, tiny scrolls; Temple of Segesta. My columns encasing secrets in their scrolls, a nod to ancient writing templates. Each scroll a small unit in a growing multiple.

> White pillars, gold pillars, wild, flying, multi-textile, green pillars.
> Clouds made by pouring plaster onto sand piles.
> Gouging,
> paint-streaking, embedding the plaster form with glass, metal and
> textile offcuts. Working fast before the plaster dries.
> City street
> bits, squashed and bent by a thousand lorries in Rio, a rusty pile of the disused
> once useful. Dull aluminium, verdigrised copper, bright new copper,
> duller brass, matt zinc, cheap tin glints like silver – silver-coated plastic.

Startle

After Pablo Neruda

The same startling Wednesday
is approaching in a repeat that is not
last Thursday, when the scene of the iced hay bales
whitening before the ancient architecture
gob-smacked me with its beauty.
The spectacle of your hands flying over the same
LED lights sunk in the pavement of the night
enchants me.
Tonight *the night is starry.*

Wild

Between two and four in the morning the Lapa tigers prowl high on the viaduct
watching the cracked tarmac of the roundabout below.

Myriads of oleander overlap it, fountaining blossom
through the welts and gashes of its disintegration.

Sun-melted gravelled tongues of tar
ooze through re-rooting banana palms

that push out fat flowers in pink stars.
Humming birds have flown ten miles from Santos Dumont airport.

They beat their wings eighty times a second to guard the cave, this entrance to the
Sugarloaf's secret interior. Its cable cars hang suspended on perpendicular granite

in a long rust-free, root-cable entanglement.
Scent of wild oregano, a low red sunset, dying pineapple palms.

Inside the cave,
at the mountain's centre,

rubber trees grow through the tables
and the marmosets serve the last caiparinhas
to the vibrations of the night capoeira.

Gradients

Are there any intervals between this slope
and the one protruding in pure white sun
on that horizon?

In white sun
these slate crags shine black,
crack a sky of crying blue.

The distant slope is measured
within their compass points
in sledge-spotted snow;
its particles fragment into glitter.

*A response to notes from Antarctic surveys at the Scott
Polar Research Institute, Cambridge*

Fragments

In the night's walls,
caterpillars of memory.

In the crowd,
the man's egg-head apple blossom.

On the journey,
blackthorn-straggled, cow parsley-clouded, larch-dangled hedge.

In their passages,
nerves flicker, resurrected light bulbs.

On the river,
a wasp's wreath lost in green.

Over hope's wide lake,
a bridge of energy.

Under the rust heads of sorrel,
a throbbing toad.

In the uncut barley field,
red tractors, yellow combines.

On the high sea barrier, over the salt marsh,
Giacometti sculptures.

In the refrigerator,
pink cartons of discovery.

On the backs of sheep, in evening sun,
stripes of milk.

Along the arterial road,
Hoovers of despair.

Life No Bigger

Life no bigger than the inside of a laurel leaf,
as pure as coal dust, as impure as gold dust.
It sways with the trees in the wind of winter,
it leans with the tree to the sea.
It boasts like the rich person's banquet,
and cries with the night cat.
It floats like the cherries on jelly.
It collapses in the throat of pain,
extends like fingers on the 'cello.

    Life as small as the inside of a laurel leaf,
    see it spin clean in the damp palm of a hand;
    watch as it zig-zags lightly along,
    boomerangs brightly,
    pulls water home,
    turns every comma into a stop,
    tunes to the rhythm of inner clocks;
    traces the curve of the sunset's glow,
    waiting, a long time, for handles to hold.

Fountain

She was there, but wraith-like, iris soft-eyed;
her dream outside these walls, her hopes a sticky layer.
Furniture around her,

    green fountains of leaves outside.

Not moving amongst the furniture.
Crescent smiles, spun-gold eyes of friends,
the colours of life condensed for keeping.

    The tip of a larch tree dangles its silhouette over a cloud.

Spring's new fullness brought sadness again.
Dry brown earth turned pink with
speckled horse chestnut dropped flower.

    Sweet evening sun palely lights a twist of trunk

and now the green hands of leaves sway and flicker
as she sits in the room's half light
watching rhododendron's candyfloss.

Put Out the Light...

Trilogy

First Act

In through this life's narrow canyon of space
flies desire at a hundred miles an hour,
surprised and laughing at arriving.

> *The engine shudders and stops*

Green, red-edged, sharp and searching,
spiralling enquiringly in the air,
alighting jerkily onto rock faces, mossy openings and mussel pools,
tearing the air with newness.

> *We see swans in fields through the train window*

There's no speed limit
I'm dizzy, can't stop seeing brightness,
exposed now, I see you,
you're right in my range.

> *Remember the rain on the verandah roof*

Expectant and beautiful,
ten degrees up from normal,
a suitable back drops for the scene.

> *Departure time 10.53, Platform Ten*

Intermission

Quiet magnets of desire, your eyes,
whitely seeing me and responding.
I'm shy too and have rolled up like a hedgehog,
expecting your rejections, not these attentions.
For you must keep all your promises
and hey this is painful, the seeing,
when I've already directed the end of the scene;
it's well-rehearsed now,
a non-porous act of art to set against the pain ...
a little humour, some catharsis, two celebrities,
but fear keeps entering the act like a whirlwind,
announcing your name.

End

My heart hangs heavy.
The angels have guns.
They crouch behind the mound of grass
below the dark pink sky.

I long for wind to blow.
I have clay dust on my shoes and see behind the broken fence
        a pine tree
still growing
in considerable beauty.

Standing as straight, I quiver,
but hold my balance,
clamping in a vice the emotions I retain.
The angels are nuns now, out from the mound.

Their eyes pin me with a Catholic heaven's rapture;
pointing their guns, they'll not fail.
I sway,
I'm giddy with vomit rising stale.

The sound comes, the bullet targets,
its pain a relief.
That hurts less, is expected.
My blood congeals into wormcasts in a few days.

Fiesole in the Bentley

Twenty years gone
and I miss you
this Saturday,
so I search in Compendium
for a trace of your published work.
I fuse the now with the then; I think vineyards, Fiesole in the Bentley,
your crazy conducting to Vivaldi
but Compendium has gone
and I remember how awful you could be,
now distance, cities and airports apart.

October

Like bluebells I remember you:
your cinnamon hair,
your indoor tortoise.

A miracle, the telephone,
it sings and grunts over Europe

disregarding geography,
—your white enamelled skin—

fetching your voice
in French to my white English room,
my burning ear.

I slide wet feet over black tiles,
leaving a snail trail, to reach the phone this Saturday.

You,
the star of surprise.

You, jumping up and down at Milan airport
in an animated crowd

misty-eyed with tears, as I arrive.
You've told them the arc of our lives.

Sucking peppermints in a Chevrolet,
we cruise and jolt in city centre drizzle.

We park and walk,
drink some beer and giggle.

You buy me a flower.
It's the reddest longest rose.

Break it
on a parked car with a barking dog.

New Door

On Tuesday I play Tosca's aria. A deep panelled door melts into a pile of wood shavings, their curls are soft and sharp, smooth skinned and clawed. This Thursday in Homebase I seek extra beading, panel pins and a tack hammer. *In need of complete renovation. Strip and re-tile adventurously.* It's bright outside and fresh, *moss removal this way.* I see gaps of new sky between plump cumulus clouds, *Wings of Peterborough,* as the newly renovated train snakes past the yellow crates of King's Cross.

Only Opera

I wear my emerald green dress that evening. Clouds curl pink above Kenwood House's Palladian cream. I'd sewn it in a sun-soaked ward of the Royal Free Hospital. It is August and so hot your clothes stick to your skin. Clumps of here and there grass grow through the dry earth and young ducks flap and splash as we eat our picnic. Your friend wears a linen suit and Panama. He's put on weight and walks like the White Rabbit. We stand for five minutes entranced by *Tosca*. The soprano flings her arms high, in crescendo, over the light-dotted lake, at the same moment as a goose flies over. She throws her notes to us and we receive them as pure emotion, lying propped on our arms by the line of food kiosks. Now stars, the moon, pierce and scatter the ultramarine sky. We de-crumb the rugs and watch the procession of Bergman figures in the night exit.

January

At Maggi's house it was seagulls throwing their cries across chimneypots and Maggi and James stepping singing into the morning. And Stephanie the blue fairy stepping out a surprise package from the sweet pink curve of her period house. Maggi's mantlepieces bedecked for Christmas and a handsome fish lying in ritual death for us. As we eat my words are picked frozen daisies spread meadow-wide under night's sky. Frozen by feeling. Frozen by feeling your eyes while life jumped with electricity round us. The chasm of feeling the seagulls flying screaming our white hands warm marble on her mantelpiece.

A Table Separates Us

A table separates us;
I don't know if it's melamine or pine,
for your sea-eyes mesmerise mine.

You shy horse-like when I offer you scent
of eucalyptus from the centre vase;
you stay at the top of your pylon,
I canter breathless on white clover ground.

Going home, perhaps a thousand words later,
in the quiet night of laurel leaves, unbudded rose,
I want to smell your skin, touch your eyes... but don't.

Fifteen Hours in Sifnos

From behind the massive night bone of mountain
the sun's un-cracked yolk slips its perfect form
over earth's contour, into sky.

The silent mountain
glows pink, aroused, announces
the blue and white Sifnos day

in which we walk six shining-sea miles
on a tiny mountain track to Kastro, ancient capital.
You're looking good today in electric blue.

Around us
the heady scent of wild basil, oregano, thyme.
The roofs, first mountain-strewn, now close, are balled

in perfect domes, blue on white, in anticipation of volcanoes.
Clusters of tiny churches, white and blue too, emit a scent of
    frankincense
and in their cool insides we intrude on precious ikons,

gilded for private reverence. An organ plays.
These rough-hewn walkways are carved from the mountain.
Through white arches, the blue surprise of the Greek sea.

At lunch we share tiropita,
feta, olives, tomatoes and the generous
free dessert. Warmed by wine

I find an azure brooch
in an Aegean doll's house-shop.
Seven Cycladic cats swamp us

with their climbing, purring,
furry welcome when we get home to Sifnaika.

The sea laps milk and blue in and away,
splashes the moon's gentle light, spreading it
in tiny sea-horse crests.

We watch the ferry come in at Kamares,
dots of light flash
in hectic green/blue coda,
as lorries spew out on cue.

You Make Me Feel Brand New

And what if an entirely new sensation struck
at each intercontinental railway station;

glittered and fast-flickered my wrist veins,
my femur and my pancreas,

splattered my aortic valve,
splintered my cranium,

dispersed my shoulder blades in bougainvillea fragments
over Bologna's beautiful Alidosi bridge? Would I still rear

as your thrown lassoes perfectly gird me?
Then you stand on the filigree balustrade of Verona

surrounded by lotus flowers, lotus flowers.

I have thrust and wriggled out of my old form
and left its skin mottled and crisp

in wet snake grass.
I am new, forms welded, muscles toned.

You gaze down at me from the precipice.
I shine you the thousand lights of the Zürich See.

Salthouse Swans

At the height of the hawthorn bush
in horizontal wing-hung line

white

across this path
three swans fly between me and the sea.

From the window, the shape of the sea pool
is a hide of leather stretched over the land.

The marshes with web-printed mud

shine

and two black swans

loosen their necks into Ss and hearts
in graceful trance of courtship.

Now the moon edges the waves' rearing
with light.

We stand on the stones of the shore;
The sea is like our heartbeat you say.

Our hearts beat as waves come in
as quiet and quick as death.

Ice Moon

I pull back from falling into the rocked crevice of love
by girding my loins with a cloth
of words soaked in wax and bitumen.

I skate-dance on ice, a solitary star,
backgrounded by Canary Wharf's skyline.
I dazzle, my feet spark, they're hung with bells.

You watch from every corner in turn, unimpressed,
eating ice cream.
While the Thames tide turns, questions flash crossette fireworks
      on the horizon.

Will the famous bridge rise?
Is the moon full? Are you ready? Do you want another one?

More poetry published by SurVision Books

Noelle Kocot. *Humanity*
(New Poetics: USA)
ISBN 978-1-9995903-0-7

Ciaran O'Driscoll. *The Speaking Trees*
(New Poetics: Ireland)
ISBN 978-1-9995903-1-4

Helen Ivory. *Maps of the Abandoned City*
(New Poetics: England)
ISBN 978-1-912963-04-1

Elin O'Hara Slavick. *Cameramouth*
(New Poetics: USA)
ISBN 978-1-9995903-4-5

John W. Sexton. *Inverted Night*
(New Poetics: Ireland)
ISBN 978-1-912963-05-8

Afric McGlinchey. *Invisible Insane*
(New Poetics: Ireland)
ISBN 978-1-9995903-3-8

Anatoly Kudryavitsky. *Stowaway*
(New Poetics: Ireland)
ISBN 978-1-9995903-2-1

Tim Murphy. *The Cacti Do Not Move*
(New Poetics: Ireland)
ISBN 978-1-912963-07-2

Tony Kitt. *The Magic Phlute*
(New Poetics: Ireland)
ISBN 978-1-912963-08-9

Clayre Benzadón. *Liminal Zenith*
(New Poetics: USA)
ISBN 978-1-912963-11-9

Thomas Townsley. *Tangent of Ardency*
(New Poetics: USA)
ISBN 978-1-912963-15-7

Matthew Geden. *Fruit*
(New Poetics: Ireland)
ISBN 978-1-912963-16-4

Marc Vincenz. *Einstein Fledermaus*
(New Poetics: USA)
ISBN 978-1-912963-20-1

George Kalamaras. *That Moment of Wept*
ISBN 978-1-9995903-7-6

Anton Yakovlev. *Chronos Dines Alone*
(Winner of James Tate Poetry Prize 2018)
ISBN 978-1-912963-01-0

Bob Lucky. *Conversation Starters in a Language No One Speaks*
(Winner of James Tate Poetry Prize 2018)
ISBN 978-1-912963-00-3

Christopher Prewitt. *Paradise Hammer*
(Winner of James Tate Poetry Prize 2018)
ISBN 978-1-9995903-9-0

Mikko Harvey & Jake Bauer. *Idaho Falls*
(Winner of James Tate Poetry Prize 2018)
ISBN 978-1-912963-02-7

Tony Bailie. *Mountain Under Heaven*
(Winner of James Tate Poetry Prize 2019)
ISBN 978-1-912963-09-6

Nicholas Alexander Hayes. *Amorphous Organics*
(Winner of James Tate Poetry Prize 2019)
ISBN 978-1-912963-10-2

John Bradley. *Spontaneous Mummification*
(Winner of James Tate Poetry Prize 2019)
ISBN 978-1-912963-13-3

John Thomas Allen. *Rolling in the Third Eye*
(Winner of James Tate Poetry Prize 2019)
ISBN 978-1-912963-15-7

Gary Glauber. *The Covalence of Equanimity*
(Winner of James Tate Poetry Prize 2019)
ISBN 978-1-912963-12-6

Charles Kell. *Pierre Mask*
(Winner of James Tate Poetry Prize 2019)
ISBN 978-1-912963-19-5

Alan Elyshevitz. *Mortal Hours*
(Winner of James Tate Poetry Prize 2020)
ISBN 978-1-912963-21-8

Maria Grazia Calandrone. *Fossils*
Translated from Italian
(New Poetics: Italy)
ISBN 978-1-9995903-6-9

Sergey Biryukov. *Transformations*
Translated from Russian
(New Poetics: Russia)
ISBN 978-1-9995903-5-2

Alexander Korotko. *Irrazionalismo*
Translated from Russian
(New Poetics: Ukraine)
ISBN 978-1-912963-06-5

Anton G. Leitner. *Selected Poems 1981–2015*
Translated from German
ISBN 978-1-9995903-8-3

message-door: An Anthology of Contemporary Surrealist Poetry from Russia (bilingual)
Edited and translated from Russian by Anatoly Kudryavitsky
ISBN 978-1-912963-17-1

Seeds of Gravity: An Anthology of Contemporary Surrealist Poetry from Ireland
Edited by Anatoly Kudryavitsky
ISBN 978-1-912963-18-8

All our books are available to order via
http://survisionmagazine.com/books.htm

www.ingramcontent.com/pod-product-compliance
Lightning Source LLC
Chambersburg PA
CBHW061310040426
42444CB00010B/2584